You Have No Carbon Copy
By Racheal Odoy

Giant Publishing Company
Lincoln, Nebraska USA

2020 by Racheal Odoy

Published by Giant Publishing Company
Post Office Box 6455
Lincoln, NE 68506
www.giantpublishingcompany.com

Printed in the United States of America

All scriptures are from the King James Version of the Bible, unless otherwise noted.

ISBN: 978-0-9995873-6-2

Odoy, Racheal
You Have No Carbon Copy
Non-fiction/Racheal Odoy
    1. Non-fiction-Christianity
    2. Bible commentary
    3. Self-help

Also by Racheal Odoy:

You Need a Jonathan
Copyright 2018

I and My Seed will Thrive
Copyright 2019

I dedicate this book to my best friend and loving husband Larry Odoy, and our children, who continually support me in this journey of spreading the gospel through writing books. May God give you long life and more blessings.

Table of Contents

Introduction

Fingerprints are usually used to identify people. It's amazing that even identical twins have different fingerprints. The more I think about it, the more I give God all the glory and honor - how he created the human race all the same, but yet very different. Every feature on the human body looks the same as the next person's, but not identical. It is very easy for someone to judge you by looks, even when they know nothing about you and have never spoken to you. Being different and unique is good, because there will never be another person like you. You may look like one of your relatives, yet still you are not them and you will never be them, even when you copy what they do, eat, wear, or how they speak.

Take a good look at yourself in the mirror and appreciate who you are, love you and purpose to make yourself happy. You can never give what you do not have. Stop working too hard to please other people; you can never reach their expectations. The truth is that we are all different in personalities, appearances, preferences and even experiences. You may have been in the same place with someone, but both of you will end up sharing your experiences differently.

You are unique and you will never have a carbon copy of you.

Ephesians 2:10 - For we are his workmanship, created in Christ Jesus unto good works, which God hath before ordained that we should walk in them.

You are going to enjoy reading this book. There is so much about yourself that you probably had overlooked, or never knew. This book will open your eyes to the truth within you that connect to the outer you. Be ready to be empowered how to make a difference in your life and build a legacy that will help so many to come after you. It's high time you stopped thinking less of yourself than you are; rise and protect you, the original copy.

The person who greatly inspired me to write this book was my good friend Linda Falls, who went to be with the lord at eighty years of age on June 1st, 2019. She was a woman of faith, and during her last days on earth, a week before she died, she shared with me about self-identity. She told me of how she managed to stay a born-again Christian for so many years amidst all the challenges she went through. She was a single mother who struggled and made sure that her children were provided for each and every day. Linda's faith always mesmerized me. She survived cancer twice, and even when she was attacked again by cancer of the throat, the doctors' report did not threaten her. She kept on preaching to the doctors, nurses and janitors. The moment someone entered her room they would be sure to hear her talk about Jesus. She had a smile on her face all the time, to a point that the doctors who were attending to her kept making comments like, 'We have never seen anyone like her; she knows she has cancer, but she is full of joy.'

Linda was indeed unique.

Poem

Briski loved herself so much, that every morning she went to the mirror and admired herself.
She would turn all sides, and make sure everything looked perfect for the day.
Throughout the day she kept going back and forth to her special spot to assure herself that everything was okay.
However, Briski had one challenge; there was this guy who was bigger than her, and always looked at her as a nobody. And the moment she would come across him, she would put her head down. This guy, Lofy, enjoyed looking at Briski walk away in fear. All it had to take was for Lofy to look at Briski, and she freaked out. This went on for so many years.
One day, Briski went to her master and asked if she could be taken far away from Lofy, but the master said, 'No!' He said, 'I love you both, and I do not want to lose either of you.'
Day and night, Briski got miserable, until she got fed up.

'The day of me becoming new has come,' said Briski.
'I will go to my mirror. I know it will give me the right answer.'
Looking in the mirror, Briski saw someone very identical to her, but the only difference was, this other person was bigger.

'Yes! Yes! This is it. I am bigger!' shouted Briski.

She went past Lofy, wagging her tail with no fear.

'What happened?' asked Lofy. 'Briski is very bold this morning.'

Lofy tried to bring his looks, but Briski was not moved. She went on the whole day very happy, and even started playing by herself.

Lofy asked her if he could join in the game. Briski said, 'Come if you want to.'

They became friends. Briski put her fear away and started living happy.

Briski knew she was different from Lofy and she had to be herself.

Briski's mind changed that one morning when she looked in the mirror and made a decision to accept who she was, and never allow Lofy to intimidate her. She was bold and courageous.

Briski the kitty cat became friends with Lofy the dog.

A cat can never be a dog and a dog can never be a cat.

There are questions people usually ask themselves when they are going through a time of trial and searching for identity. It is a very challenging time of life, and if somebody gets no help, nor opens up to another person, they end up living a lost life, with no purpose. They find themselves in the company of wrong people who drag them down with them, and as a result some commit suicide, others are killed in gang violence, while others choose to be lonely and useless till their time of death. I am propelled to write down these questions while answering them, to help that person out there to rise up and get self-identity for life to make a meaning to them and the people they care about.

Chapter 1: Who am I?

Have you ever asked yourself this question? If you have not done so, then you need to, because it will bring you to actualization of who you are and self-identity. This question is asked by so many, and yet very few get the answer. In most cases people tend to please others, or go miles to do things for others, and they forget themselves. It's because the biggest percentage of people seek out favors from others in order to be accepted.

This is very common among teenagers and youths when they are seeking for identity. They usually desire to get a friend or get into a group that will accept them. The only problem is they never get to accept themselves, but will do everything to get a sense of belonging among their peers. That's why it is very important for every parent to help their child build self-confidence and teach them how to believe in themselves. By doing so they would have saved the child from making wrong choices of friends. If you are a parent, always speak to your child and affirm to them how valuable, smart, brave, good-looking, strong, and courageous they are. This helps create in them a personality of never following the crowd, but always taking a bold step in every decision they make.

It is next to impossible to live a happy life when you do not know who you are. Other people doing better than you should never intimidate you or cause you fear. Let it be a challenge you take up to make things better in your life.

First and foremost, avoid living in denial and accept the things you see in you. This will reveal all that needs to be changed, or do without. Learn to embrace the good in you; this will make others admire you. Be yourself, and that person you admire should be an encouragement because you cannot be them. Even when you copy what they do, wear, or how they speak, it will eventually frustrate you, since that is not you. It is not worth putting in so much effort to be like someone else, yet you can make yourself become that person others can admire. This is like women wearing makeup. Ten women can wear the same makeup, yet look different, and it's because we all have different skin tones. Even though they layer up the makeup, still the shape of the lips, the eye color, and the shape of the nose is different. What I am trying to bring to your attention is, you need not to be someone else; be yourself and accept who you are. It begins by loving the way God created you and taking good care of yourself. Never let someone else rob you of your identity by making you into what they want you to be in order to fit their expectations. That can only cause you pain and self-rejection, and as a result, you will be living a fake and miserable life. God created you in his image and likeness, so you deserve the best, and God gives the best.

If you lost your identity or have not yet known who you are, I have good news for you. This book is going to open your eyes to the reality of who you are. It's time to get yourself back.

1 Timothy 4:4 - For every creature of God is good, and nothing to be refused, if it be received with thanksgiving:

Ephesians 2:10 - For we are his workmanship, created in Christ Jesus unto good works, which God hath before ordained that we should walk in them.

Psalm 139:14 - I will praise thee; for I am fearfully and wonderfully made: marvellous are thy works; and that my soul knoweth right well.

Chapter 2: Where do I come from?

This question is commonly asked by people within themselves - rarely does someone outwardly ask this question. If so, there are few cases. Even you reading this, there's a time you asked yourself this question. It was probably sparked by a thought of, 'Where does my surname originate from? Who were my ancestors?' I have come across people who even go to the extent of going for a genealogy test. It has become very common for people to get a DNA test to prove their right identity.

The more someone asks themselves this question, the more they become restless. Some give themselves nicknames for identity purposes. First of all, this question cannot be answered well if you don't know who you are. Take a minute now, go to the mirror, and have a good look at yourself. As you do that, ask yourself these questions: "Who is that other person in the mirror? What does she/he have that can help motivate him/her?" You need to love what you see, and that is your image. Every bit of yourself is unique, if you did not know that. There is nobody on earth who looks exactly like you. The moment you accept everything you see about yourself, then you have reached the place of answering this question: "Where do I come from?"

There are cases where some people give themselves names, looking at where they come from, and they are not proud of it. So, they identify themselves by a place, and acquire a name to feel good about themselves. But the fact remains that the place you came from exists, though you may not want to identify with it.

One day a certain lady came for counseling, asking herself this question, "Where do I come from?" She didn't believe in herself, even in circumstances where others believed in her, and it's because she never knew her father. Considering her status is society, she still felt very lonely and lost.

If you happen to be bothered so much by where you came from, it is better you take it upon yourself and make a difference by being a pursuer and going for the best. Meaning, whatever you do, give it your best and be successful in it. As time goes on, you will want to associate with where you came from, knowing that you are the person that has created the difference amongst all. You can't change the past, but you can change the future, and your past becomes history that makes a good story to encourage others.

Genesis 1:27 - So God created man in his own image, in the image of God created he him; male and female created he them.

Jeremiah 1:5 - Before I formed thee in the belly I knew thee; and before thou camest forth out of the womb I sanctified thee, and I ordained thee a prophet unto the nations.

John 1:12 - But as many as received him, to them gave he power to become the sons of God, even to them that believe on his name.

Ephesians 1:5 - Having predestinated us unto the adoption of children by Jesus Christ to himself, according to the good pleasure of his will.

1 Peter 2:9 - But ye are a chosen generation, a royal priesthood, an holy nation, a peculiar people; that ye should shew forth the praises of him who hath called you out of darkness into his marvellous light.

Chapter 3: What is my purpose for living?

Have you asked yourself this question before? If yes, then you are on your way to success. And if no, then it's high time you asked. This is a question that needs to be asked by everyone, because it gives you direction to where you are heading in life.

Successful people always know their true identity, then work towards making a legacy. There can only be one you on earth; nobody can ever be you, though they may try to be like you. You are unique, and the qualities that make you are within you, where no one can get them to work, unless you make a decision to make yourself be challenged by you.

Since we are all uniquely created by God, it may require you to do different things until you discover where your greatest strength is. And there are those who God gifted in different things and they are good at almost everything they do, yet others can hardly do more than one thing. That brings me back to you being unique. You do not need to imitate what someone else is doing. It's important to discover you. It's good to be inspired by someone, but they cannot get you to discover you. I have come across some people who desire to sing because they feel motivated by a certain musician, but when they try to sing, you can tell it's not their calling; their music does not sound good at all, and their voices are not good. You may not know how to sing, but that does not mean that you are not good at something else. You just need to discover yourself. What you cannot do well should never stop you from trying something else. You will eventually discover what you are good at. When you do, give it your best, and through that, you will become very successful, and an inspiration to many.

Your purpose for living is to make a difference in your life by being different from everyone else, in order to have a positive impact in the lives of those around you and those far from you. In everything you do, a positive attitude is very important for motivation and perfection.

Look at it this way. When a child is learning to walk, he/she falls multiple times, but that child does not give up. They keep standing up, and sometimes hold on to any object close to them for support. They do it over and over until they are able to stand and walk on their own. Not long after that they gain stamina and even start running. Why? Inside of every child, there is a potential to walk and run, but it's a process of discovering it, trying it, and soon enough they are good at it.

You have the potential of success inside of you. You can do it and you can make it. Do not ever allow fear to stop you from discovering the real you who was created for a purpose. When a child starts to stand and takes their first step, the parent cheers on and encourages him/her to do it more.

Start taking a step of faith and purpose to make an impression before the father (God). He will cheer you up by causing the right people to identify you for connection. Such people are known as destiny helpers, who are meant to propel that which you are carrying to the next level.

After discovering what you are good at, do not stop simply because no one is recognizing you. Keep on keeping on, and as you do it, you will gain more skill, and in a blink of an eye you are a professional. In no time, people will discover you and want your product, others will desire to support you, while others will want to learn from you. That's how you get to know the purpose for your living (creating a legacy). Remember: winners never quit, and quitters never win. Also, falling is not failing. You can make it, in Jesus' mighty name.

Philippians 4:13 - I can do all things through Christ which strengtheneth me.

2 Corinthians 5:7 - For we walk by faith, not by sight.

Proverbs 20:5 - The purposes of a person's heart are deep waters, but one who has insight draws them out.

Proverbs 19:21 - Many are the plans in a person's heart, but it is the Lord's purpose that prevails.

Job 42:2 - I know that you can do all things; no purpose of yours can be thwarted.

Chapter 4: Who can help me?

Guess who is the best person to help you? That's you. After you have come to a place of acceptance and self-identity, it becomes very easy to help yourself rise up. It starts from within; your mind must purpose to see change, then your heart determines to work at it. It will be very easy for you to identify who has your best interest. God usually aligns different people in our paths to help us, though it is always upon the one who needs help to identify the right person.

An example: if you are sick, you go to see a physician. All it takes is for you to start feeling your body becoming strange to you. A person without cancer cannot go for chemotherapy.

You have to get to a point when you can identify what your problem is to seek for help. It may not necessarily be a problem, but a weakness. There's always that person whom I call your destiny helper. God will lead your way.

It's high time you got tired of that situation and desperately reach out for help. Start by confidently praying about it and boldly taking steps that are going to help you get out of that situation.

In Genesis 27:40, Isaac told his son Esau after his brother Jacob had taken his blessing that when a time comes and he is tired, he shall break the yoke off his shoulder. At that point Esau was angry with Jacob for what he did. However much he pursued after his brother Jacob, he would not take the blessing back. He had to free himself from anger and break the curse off of him.

Genesis 27:40 - And by thy sword shalt thou live, and shalt serve thy brother; and it shall come to pass when thou shalt have the dominion, that thou shalt break his yoke from off thy neck.

In Genesis 33:1-4, Jacob meets his brother Esau in fear of his life, knowing what he had done in the past. But Esau did not harm him at all, but embraced him, which shows that by the time the two brothers met, Esau was not angry at Jacob. He was prosperous. So, Esau broke the yoke off his shoulder.

Genesis 33:1-4 - And Jacob lifted up his eyes, and looked, and, behold, Esau came, and with him four hundred men. And he divided the children unto Leah, and unto Rachel, and unto the two handmaids. And he put the handmaids and their children foremost, and Leah and her children after, and Rachel and Joseph hindermost. And he passed over before them, and bowed himself to the ground seven times, until he came near to his brother. And Esau ran to meet him, and embraced him, and fell on his neck, and kissed him: and they wept.

Your success and prosperity are waiting for you; however, you must get tired of being in the same place, and stop grieving and feeling pity for yourself. Rise up and help yourself. You start it and more doors open up, leading more destiny helpers your way.

Habakkuk 2:3 - For the vision is yet for an appointed time, but at the end it shall speak, and not lie: though it tarry, wait for it; because it will surely come, it will not tarry.

Isaiah 46:10 - Declaring the end from the beginning, and from ancient times the things that are not yet done, saying, My counsel shall stand, and I will do all my pleasure.

Chapter 5: Where is my Helper?

Your help comes from the Lord. God will always put the right people in your path to help you. Seek the Lord more, put your trust in him and move by faith. By taking the first step of rising up to help yourself, it will be easy for you to meet that person divinely meant to help you.

Psalm 46:1-2 - God is our refuge and strength, a very present help in trouble. Therefore, will not we fear, though the earth be removed, and though the mountains be carried into the midst of the sea.

Isaiah 41:10 - Fear thou not; for I am with thee: be not dismayed; for I am thy God: I will strengthen thee; yea, I will help thee; yea, I will uphold thee with the right hand of my righteousness.

Psalm 54:4 - Behold, God is mine helper: the Lord is with them that uphold my soul.

Chapter 6: David, the man of identity

The right man in the Bible who had an identity that could not be duplicated or go unnoticed was David. And the first time we hear about him was when prophet Samuel went to anoint a king from the household of Jesse, and none of the other seven children were anointed except David, who was the youngest and absent at the arrival of prophet Samuel. He was called out and anointed. That clearly shows that his destiny was marked to be a king from childhood, though it had to take the servant of God to anoint him and separate him from the rest. After that we see David starting to walk towards his destiny when he went to take food for his brothers who were at a camp in the valley of Elah fighting the Philistines.

David's instructions from his father were to take food and return home to his father with news on how his brothers were faring. But because of the anointing which was upon David, it was the time when God had divinely appointed for him to confront the giant (Goliath) who was threatening the army of Israel. That is how David started his walk to the destined position of being the king of Israel.

David was a small boy of seventeen years, looked down upon by his brothers, yet anointed, bold and fearless. His inner man was prepared to lift the name of the Lord high in any situation. When David heard Goliath, the champion of Gath, speak, he was compelled to ask:

1 Samuel 17:26-28 - And David spake to the men that stood by him, saying, What shall be done to the man that killeth this Philistine, and taketh away the reproach from Israel? for who is this uncircumcised Philistine, that he should defy the armies of the living God? And the people answered him after this manner, saying, So shall it be done to the man that killeth him. And Eliab his eldest brother heard when he spake unto the men; and Eliab's anger was kindled against David, and he said, Why camest thou down hither? and with whom hast thou left those few sheep in the wilderness? I know thy pride, and the naughtiness of thine heart; for thou art come down that thou mightest see the battle.

Though David's eldest brother got angry hearing David ask what would be done for the man who confronts Goliath, David did not allow that to stop him from finding out how to fight Goliath, and the reward the person would be given.

1 Samuel 17:29-37 - And David said, What have I now done? Is there not a cause? And he turned from him toward another, and spake after the same manner: and the people answered him again after the former manner. And when the words were heard which David spake, they rehearsed them before Saul: and he sent for him. And David said to Saul, Let no man's heart fail because of him; thy servant will go and fight with this Philistine. And Saul said to David, Thou art not able to go against this Philistine to fight with him: for thou art but a youth, and he a man of war from his youth. And David said unto Saul, Thy servant kept his father's sheep, and there came a lion, and a bear, and took a lamb out of the flock: And I went out after him, and smote him, and delivered it out of his mouth: and when he arose against me, I caught him by his beard, and smote him, and slew him. Thy servant slew both the lion and the bear: and this uncircumcised Philistine shall be as one of them, seeing he hath defied the armies of the living God. David said moreover, The Lord that delivered me out of the paw of the lion, and out of the paw of the bear, he will deliver me out of the hand of this Philistine. And Saul said unto David, Go, and the Lord be with thee.

As a born-again Christian, you should have an experience to always refer to when it comes to going for warfare. There is so much out there for you, but it will take you to stand up, not listening to naysayers, and not giving up so that you can see victory. Always stand as you, not someone else.

David refused to wear Saul's armor to go confront Goliath, although Saul was king.

1 Samuel 17:38-40 - And Saul armed David with his armor, and he put an helmet of brass upon his head; also he armed him with a coat of mail. And David girded his sword upon his armor, and he assayed to go; for he had not proved it. And David said unto Saul, I cannot go with these; for I have not proved them. And David put them off him. And he took his staff in his hand, and chose him five smooth stones out of the brook, and put them in a shepherd's bag which he had, even in a scrip; and his sling was in his hand: and he drew near to the Philistine.

David knew who he was, and Saul's experience was not his experience. Definitely, Saul's armor could not fit him.

You should never go to war with another person's experience. It is important to dress appropriately according to what you are about to confront. When David tried on Saul's armor, his statement was 'I cannot go with these, for I have not proved them.' And he took them off.

Be yourself in everything you are doing; avoid being someone else. Each one of us is created uniquely with different abilities and skills. You may have passed through the same situations, but each one of you handled it differently, which shows you are not the same.

Saul had an experience of going to war, but at this time he was full of fear, desperation and worry, to the point that when David approached him, he was ready to let him go fight since he had no other option. One thing Saul didn't know was that this was David's divine appointment to be lifted.

A situation may seem desperate and cause restlessness in others, but for you who trusts in God and walks by faith, not by sight, it is an opportunity for you to be lifted up by allowing your faith work for you.

Romans 10:11 - For the scripture saith, Whosoever believeth on him shall not be ashamed.

2 Corinthians 5:7 - For we walk by faith, not by sight.

When David went down to meet Goliath, he carried with him what he knew to use best and get victory. All he carried was a staff, stones, bag, and sling.

1 Samuel 17:40 - And he took his staff in his hand, and chose him five smooth stones out of the brook, and put them in a shepherd's bag which he had, even in a scrip; and his sling was in his hand: and he drew near to the Philistine.

It's very important to know your strength and weaknesses so that when you get in situations, you know what to do without the compromise of approaching it like someone else. Walk with boldness, in power and victory, knowing that God is with you in all and will never forsake you. No matter how hard things may seem, you will come through. Learn not to depend on people, but God. People can easily walk away from you in fear or in search of their own desires.

Ephesians 3:12 – In whom we have boldness and access with confidence by the faith of him.

Hebrews 13:5 - Let your conversation be without covetousness; and be content with such things as ye have: for he hath said, I will never leave thee, nor forsake thee.

1 Peter 5:7 - Casting all your care upon him; for he careth for you.

Psalm 37:3 - Trust in the LORD, and do good; so shalt thou dwell in the land, and verily thou shalt be fed.

Proverbs 3:5-6 - Trust in the LORD with all thine heart; and lean not unto thine own understanding. In all thy ways acknowledge him, and he shall direct thy paths.

David believed in himself and knew he had experience with what he carried to fight Goliath, and above all, he completely put his trust in God. Goliath despised him, but it did not cause any fear in him.

1 Samuel 17:43-46 - And the Philistine said unto David, Am I a dog, that thou comest to me with staves? And the Philistine cursed David by his gods. And the Philistine said to David, Come to me, and I will give thy flesh unto the fowls of the air, and to the beasts of the field. Then said David to the Philistine, Thou comest to me with a sword, and with a spear, and with a shield: but I come to thee in the name of the Lord of hosts, the God of the armies of Israel, whom thou hast defied. This day will the Lord deliver thee into mine hand; and I will smite thee, and take thine head from thee; and I will give the carcases of the host of the Philistines this day unto the fowls of the air, and to the wild beasts of the earth; that all the earth may know that there is a God in Israel.

What you say determines what manifests. (Confession is possession.) David spoke of his victory before he fought. That gave him victory in the spiritual realm, so that when he swung his sling with the stone, he hit Goliath on the head and he fell down.

Start confessing great things about yourself and avoid speaking negatively. You might have found yourself in situations that you never desired to be in, and maybe ended up speaking negatively, making statements like: I don't think I will ever make it, I am tired of life, nothing I do prospers, all people hate me, I hate marriage, I am a nobody, I am poor, everyone hates me. Such statements are literally attracting all kinds of spirits that start claiming your destiny and causing calamities, one after another.

Proverbs 18:21 - Death and life are in the power of the tongue: and they that love it shall eat the fruit thereof.

Proverbs 13:3 - He that keepeth his mouth keepeth his life: but he that openeth wide his lips shall have destruction.

Matthew 12:37 - For by thy words thou shalt be justified, and by thy words thou shalt be condemned.

There are situations that come your way and are meant to cause elevation in your life, but the way you handle them will determine whether you win or lose. Great men and women fall and rise. Falling is recorded as an experience and a lesson.

Do not give up on yourself no matter how many times you fall.

Proverbs 24:16 - For a just man falleth seven times, and riseth up again: but the wicked shall fall into mischief.

Isaiah 52:2 - Shake thyself from the dust; arise, and sit down, O Jerusalem: loose thyself from the bands of thy neck, O captive daughter of Zion.

Ezra 10:4 - Arise; for this matter belongeth unto thee: we also will be with thee: be of good courage, and do it.

Chapter 7: The original you

We are all created unique, and different in almost everything inside and outside which makes life beautiful. We complement one another and contribute to the society differently.

It is unfortunate that some people exchange their originality and become someone else they admire and want to be like, not knowing that their uniqueness is meant to create a difference in the community.

Nobody can be you and you can never be someone else. Never fear seeing someone trying to copy what you are doing, because you have a unique DNA that identifies you from anyone else. You are you, and anybody trying to be you is a carbon copy of you, which looks totally different from the original. It's high time you embraced, loved, and uplifted you.

Psalm 139:14-16 - I will praise thee; for I am fearfully and wonderfully made: marvellous are thy works; and that my soul knoweth right well. My substance was not hid from thee, when I was made in secret, and curiously wrought in the lowest parts of the earth. Thine eyes did see my substance, yet being inperfect; and in thy book all my members were written, which in continuance were fashioned, when as yet there was none of them.

Aspects of the original you

Appearance

This is where it all begins. If you ever look at yourself and start comparing your appearance to others, wanting to look like someone else, then know that is an identity crisis. Some people go to an extent of doing plastic surgery in order to change to what makes them feel good and accepted. Even though the outside is changed, if the inside does not come to acceptance, then the outside looks will continue being an obstacle to success. It does not matter how others look at you; the most important person to look at you, is you. If you accept who you are, it will be easy for you to take care of yourself. It is good to appreciate how others look, but they are not you. Take a few minutes and go find a mirror. Look at yourself, and if you happen to see something on you that does not impress you, such as the shape of your nose, eye color, hair type, lips, or ears, the first thing you should say is: I love the way God created me, unique and good-looking. Acceptance is self-empowering; it gives you boldness and courage.

No one will ever put you down or intimidate you, as long as you believe in yourself.

Read this loudly:

Father, I thank you for who I am. I love the way I look - my smile, eyes, nose, size, hair and my ears. I am going to take care of myself and make my family very proud. In Jesus' mighty name, amen.

Do you want to know something? Instead of you wanting to be someone else, work on you by taking very good care of yourself. Others will admire to be like you.

Values and beliefs

Beliefs are those things taken to be very important, and are not to be contradicted. People's beliefs grow from what they see, hear, experience, read and think about. From these things they develop an opinion that they hold to be true and unmovable.

Beliefs usually develop into values as a person consistently holds onto them and makes them important.

Values are stable, long-lasting beliefs about what is important to a person. They become standards by which people order their lives and make their choices. To make clear, rational, responsible and consistent decisions, people should be in position to articulate their values.

Your beliefs develop into your values, and your values hold you accountable to your beliefs.

Where someone grew up, the society they were in, their family upbringing, religious beliefs and cultural beliefs, all greatly influence and set a pace for that person as he/she becomes a decision maker. Sometimes people change as they migrate from place to place, interacting with different people. And as they interact, there is a tendency of adopting new behaviors as they take up new values and beliefs. Even in circumstances like that, there is always that one thing someone can never compromise on or do, regardless of where they are.

As an individual, it is very important to discover who you are, however much you interact with different people. You must be in position to distinguish between what is right or wrong, what adds to you or subtracts from you, what builds you or destroys you, and how to become successful or what brings failure.

Beliefs and values should be individualistic as you see yourself progressing. Things you see as right, and hold onto as you grow, create self-identity.

You may adopt new beliefs as you interact with different people, but it should not rob you of your originality, resulting in you becoming someone else's carbon copy.

Maintaining your values and beliefs

- Avoid compromise, no matter what situation may present itself before you.
- Never be a people-pleaser, because it will drain you and take away a part of you.
- Be decisive and firm when it comes to making choices of different things.
- Never be moved by the crowd. Make personal decisions.
- Set personal limits to certain things where you know they may lead you astray.
- Set personal goals to help you grow.
- Have a personal evaluation every now and then to help you improve accordingly.
- Always look presentable no matter the place.
- Avoid being prideful; have a humble spirit.
- Never give up on what you believe in.
- Be selective in friends and the company you keep around.
- Not everyone should know everything about you. Keep your secrets.
- Above all, put God first in all that you are doing, and let prayer be your number one, each and every day.

40

Language/Accent

During growth and development, every child learns to speak, and they easily pick up words by listening and learning from those around them. It is the reason why each and every one of us speaks the way we do. However, as a child grows up, he/she continually learns new words, which they apply in their vocabulary in speech. And that also is greatly influenced by the environment.

In this globalization, there is a tendency of people migrating from one continent to another and by doing so, they tend to adapt to the language spoken by the people they find in those places. There is one important thing I have observed; when an adult migrates or moves to a different country or location where a different language is spoken from that they are familiar with, they will continue speaking their known language, however much they learn a new one. If they happen to have children from the place of immigration, they teach them the mother tongue.

This takes us back to what you read earlier on values and beliefs. Because of an individual's pride in his/her values and beliefs, they hardly forget their mother tongue.

When a person learns a language spoken by the people that he/she interacts with, they tend to have what is termed as an accent. The originals/natives of the place where the immigrant lives easily distinguish the person who has adapted to their language from the one who learned it from childhood, because the pronunciation of words is different. People who learn a new language apart from that which is not their mother tongue sound different from the natives of the place, causing an inferiority complex.

What will always give you boldness is loving who you are and what is inside of you, and accepting it. Your "now" behavior and language were formed during growth and development, yet greatly influenced by the surrounding environment. How you sound when speaking to others does not matter, especially when you know that you articulate the words. It's your boldness and presentation before others that will take you so far and present opportunities before you. Do your best to embrace other people's beliefs, especially if they are acceptable in society, and do not defile or destroy your values and beliefs that give you true identity. Don't forget that learning is a continuous curve and being linguistic (speaking more than one language) presents opportunities.

There are fifty-four countries on the African continent, and some of them have what are known as tribes, where each tribe speaks a different dialect. In France they speak French, and in Germany they speak German, yet on the African continent, it is next to impossible to find countries speaking the same language.

Looking at Uganda, my mother land: It is a home to many tribes that speak different dialects. There are fifty-six tribes and about nine indigenous communities that formally came to be recognized in the 1995 constitution, which was amended in 2005. English is the official language of Uganda. Luganda and Swahili are also widely spoken in most parts of the country. French, Arabic and German are taught in institutions of learning.

Each tribe is known to have its own residential area where they are found to be in a large number, and it is that common language they speak that keeps them together.

Within their community, there are customs, norms, values and beliefs that keep them together. This is from the rituals they perform from when a child is born and trained into adulthood, marriage ceremonies and death ceremonies. Within their communities, all seem to be okay and expected, yet if another person from a different tribe migrates to a community which is not their tribe, they find everything unique, different, and strange.

Of late, there are intermarriages, where a person from a different tribe marries someone of a different tribe, and by so doing they are forced to learn one another's language. They may not speak it fluently, but they try, since it is the only way they are able to live in harmony and have a sense of belonging.

It does not matter where you find yourself; the most important thing is never to lose self, even though you end up adapting to the language spoken in that particular place. Always live to make a difference, and speak to make a point.

In the book of Esther, we read about a woman who was known as Hadassah, taken on the king's orders (king Ahasuerus) after the king's wife, queen Vashti, refused to present herself before the guests as commanded by the king. She was sent out of the palace, and a royal decree was passed to gather all fair young virgins and put them under the custody of Hege, the king's chamberlain, keeper of the women, for purification and preparation, so they could be presented before the king, for him to pick one that pleased him and be the next queen.

Hadassah had been brought up by Mordecai, a Jew, who had been carried away from Jerusalem as a captive, along with Jeconiah king of Judah.

Nebuchadnezzar the king of Babylon had forcibly taken many of the Jews from their homeland.

Hadassah grew up in a foreign land, but was taught well by Mordecai about who she was, and the values and beliefs of the Jews. So, when she was taken with the rest of the virgins, he cautioned her to call herself Esther, not Hadassah any more. And out of all the virgins, it was Esther who was selected by the king; she became the queen. One thing she never forgot were her values and beliefs. When a time came, and Haman the Agagite planned to assassinate all the Jews, it was Esther who went ahead, giving instructions to the Jews on how to save their lives by commanding them to go into prayer and fasting for three days. By the time she presented herself before the king, she had favor and used wisdom, so that the tables were turned against Haman the enemy of the Jews, and the gallows he had made to hang Mordecai on were used to hang him, instead.

So, any place you find yourself in, no matter the values and beliefs of the people there, stick to yours and respect theirs, however much you adapt to their language. Esther knew who she was, and with wisdom she was able to save the entire nation from being assassinated. You are placed in a position for a purpose.

History (past experiences)

An experience makes you an expert.

Romans 8:28 - And we know that all things work together for good to them that love God, to them who are the called according to his purpose.

Your past has such a great impact on you, knowingly or unknowingly. The unfortunate thing is that it is very easy to remember all the bad experiences and forget the good. It is because when good happens, it is taken in for that moment, and hardly do people hold onto it as life goes on, except in circumstances like weddings or graduations. When someone causes you pain, you will always refer to it, and in most cases regret why you had to go through it. However, on the positive side, if every experience is treasured, good or bad, it becomes a lesson in life, depending on how you react to it. It's like college students who are supposed to attend lectures, and each time they do, they earn a point, which in the long run adds up to their scores, which is beneficial to their graduation.

After graduation, they are no longer considered as students since they are out of college. Surprisingly, some people end up having jobs or working in fields which are totally different from what they graduated in.

Success does not come because of what you went through, but rather, the opportunities presented to you and how you react to/handle them.

Every time you focus on the bad experiences you've had, chances are you may fail to handle the current opportunities you meet. People who have betrayed you act as a stepping stone for you to go higher. You are probably asking, "How?" Look back at the time you spent with them. Were you on the receiving end, or were they? Secondly, evaluate the conversation you used to have with them. Were they talking more, or did you talk more?

James 1:19 - Wherefore, my beloved brethren, let every man be swift to hear, slow to speak, slow to wrath.

When you talk too much, words become a tool of destruction, because you empower the other party. And by the way, sometimes it may not be that you talk too much, but the kind of person you keep close to you greatly determines what they bring to the table. What are they adding to you? Therefore, it is very important to be selective in the kind of friends you keep around you. There are those who only stay around to hear what you say, and constantly use it against you.

Luke 6:45 - A good man out of the good treasure of his heart bringeth forth that which is good; and an evil man out of the evil treasure of his heart bringeth forth that which is evil: for of the abundance of the heart his mouth speaketh.

Proverbs 10:19 - In the multitude of words there wanteth not sin: but he that refraineth his lips is wise.

Life itself is a classroom. Every day we learn something new, but the question you should ask yourself is, "How can I implement what I have learned?"

I have been in situations where I sacrifice so much for someone, and in a blink of an eye, that person turns against me, throwing insults at me. But that has never changed who I am. I continue helping, and one principle I go by is this: Help and expect nothing.

Let me share this brief story/testimony. I know you will learn something from it.

One day I was at church. A lady came to me with so many questions, but all she wanted me to do was to say 'yes' to everything she believed was right. She was in a relationship with a certain man for about two years, and he constantly promised to marry her. So, she had gotten to the point of getting tired. All I told her was to wait on the Lord so that he would open her eyes to certain things she did not know about this man, then she would be in a better position to decide whether she should marry him or not. Not long after that, she came complaining that he was just using her. I encouraged her to keep in prayer and attend church fellowship so that she could learn more about the principles of God. She opened up to me and told me she had never read a Bible and never spoken in tongues, and does not even know how to pray. I asked God for grace to help her, and so I took that step. She used to live in so much fear because of the voodoo items she had in her house that she got from places her friends had taken her for help. I took her through deliverance and threw out all the things that were in her house. She had things like red candles, white cloths, salt, and lots more. I taught her that God does not work through things like that, but by reading his word and praying constantly. I sacrificed so much time for her, to a point of going to her house and cooking for her, while listening to all she was carrying on her chest.

She transformed enormously. I even gave her business ideas and helped her get started. I showed her how to study the Bible. She learned to pray, speak in tongues, and she started receiving dreams and visions. One day I went to her house to pray for her, but this time she turned around and said that she was the one to pray for me. I could not understand what she was up to. As I was leaving her house, the Lord spoke to me that I should get ready; she was about to hurt me badly. That was a hard hit. So, I started withdrawing from her after the warning. It did not take long. She stopped coming to church; she stopped calling or texting. I was not surprised. She started telling other church members that she could also prophesy, see visions and interpret dreams, and told them I was not needed. She started causing division in church. I went on my knees, prayed, and asked God to deal with the situation, since the church was becoming divided. One night during Bible study, she came and said she was leaving church and never coming back. Though the Lord had prepared me, I got hurt looking at the sacrifices I had made to help her in the past months. I could hardly pray about the situation because of the pain in my heart. I started thanking God for her life, and God healed me miraculously. And, my heart was full of joy, knowing she met me and was transformed, for the glory of our living God.

What I'm trying to bring to your attention is, no matter the sacrifices you do for people, some of them will never appreciate it, but instead turn against you. Do not hold them on your heart; it limits your way forward. Let your sacrifices or help to people turn into thanksgiving to God. Holding on to pain caused by someone you loved and trusted means you have allowed that person to control your feelings and decision making, and you can even fail to pray, because you are carrying pain inside. But in all things, give thanks to God. Always ask God to strengthen you and heal you, so that your spirit can easily open up to the next person God directs in your life for help. Most importantly, never make a major decision when you are hurting or angry. Give yourself time to heal so that you can move forward.

Everything that happens in your life is for a season and a reason; take it as a class that brings promotion. Your experiences make you an expert in that specific field.

Chapter 8: The invisible you

Did you know that the real you is not seen or known by anyone? If you didn't know, then it's high time your eyes got opened as you read. People tend to describe you based on what they see and what you do, and in most cases, they are wrong. Because they start to treat you based on that, and no matter how hard you try to prove a point, their perception about you is glued in their minds.

Potential

These are abilities that may be developed leading to future success or usefulness. It all starts from knowing who you are and to what extent you go when you start to do something. The problem comes when you do not believe in yourself, but yet try to prove a point to impress others. Yet, your success depends on your wholesome you. (It starts with you, but it's never about you.)

Your potential cannot be utilized until you start envisioning yourself far from where you are. Do not allow the present unpleasant circumstances to dictate your future. Have a vision and write down what you need to happen.

Habakkuk 2:2-3 - And the Lord answered me, and said, Write the vision, and make it plain upon tables, that he may run that readeth it. For the vision is yet for an appointed time, but at the end it shall speak, and not lie: though it tarry, wait for it; because it will surely come, it will not tarry.

Go after your dream; very soon it will be actualized and visible, even without you giving an explanation. The drive should be from the inside of you, which no man sees or understands. Your worst enemy that causes failure is fear of the unknown, and the fact that it is unknown. Keep pushing to what you are envisioning, and whatever comes your way as an obstacle will be easy to overcome, since what drives you is the unseen potential. And that is called faith.

2 Timothy 1:7 - For God hath not given us the spirit of fear; but of power, and of love, and of a sound mind.

Hebrews 11:1 - Now faith is the substance of things hoped for, the evidence of things not seen.

2 Corinthians 5:7 - For we walk by faith, not by sight.

Reality vs. the invisible

At the time of actualization or making that vision come into manifestation, there are things that usually come your way which you had not prepared for. But no matter how hard you are hit, the secret of victory is to remain focused. Negativity will come your way, like people telling you how hard that business is that you are venturing in, or how it has failed for so many, or how it is next to impossible to be a success in that area. But the key is: before you even start chasing for that vision, look at who is doing a similar thing to what you are desiring to do, since it is in line with your vision. Look at their weaknesses and strengths, so that from there, you are able to build a strong and stable foundation for your vision to start moving up.

It is just like wanting to build a hotel. The first question is: have you ever stayed in different hotels, and if so, what did you like, and what didn't you like? Location is very important, and what will make people prefer to stay at your hotel, rather than the already existing one. Looking at all the nitty-gritty involved in such a business. It gives you ideas on how to get started with your project.

When sharing such a big project with people, be ready to hear the negatives. How you take them in is the most important part, because you might be discouraged if they are not properly thought about.

Usually what people say to us determines a lot of how we behave. But as long as you know who you are and what you want, it will be next to impossible for people to discourage you.

Remember, no one knows you better than you know yourself. People will describe you according to what is visible to them. Learn to keep certain things to yourself; people should not know everything about you.

Jeremiah 17: 9 - The heart is deceitful above all things, and desperately wicked: who can know it?

You can never know what is hidden in the heart of people, so whenever you are sharing things about you, be conscious of what you are saying. Otherwise, you might regret it later when the very people you trusted have betrayed you.

Secrets

I have come across people complaining that they were betrayed by the people they trusted. And it is because they never had limits to what they were telling them. In life, learn to always reserve some information for yourself and not share it with others. What you feel is personal should remain with you.

Mathew 10:36 - And a man's foes shall be they of his own household.

If the invisible you learns to keep secrets, rarely will you be betrayed.

Mathew 12:37 - For by thy words thou shalt be justified, and by thy words thou shalt be condemned.

Weaknesses

People always tend to blame themselves when they realize that it's their weakness that led them into making a mistake. The way you can realize that you have a weakness in a particular area, it's advantageous because it helps you start to work on it. And as long as you know your area of strength, put more effort in that area as you slowly work on the weakness so that you do not get disappointed. When you focus so much on your weakness, you might fail to work on your strong area which is supposed to propel you higher. Every person has their point of strength and weakness, but the difference is, the successful ones choose to focus on their strong areas.

Isaiah 40:29 - He gives strength to the weary and increases the power of the weak (New International Version).

1 Peter 5:7 - Casting all your care upon him; for he careth for you.

Philippians 4:13 - I can do all things through Christ which strengtheneth me.

Psalm 46 - God is our refuge and strength, a very present help in trouble. Therefore, will not we fear, though the earth be removed, and though the mountains be carried into the midst of the sea; Though the waters thereof roar and be troubled, though the mountains shake with the swelling thereof. Selah. There is a river, the streams whereof shall make glad the city of God, the holy place of the tabernacles of the most High. God is in the midst of her; she shall not be moved: God shall help her, and that right early. The heathen raged, the kingdoms were moved: he uttered his voice, the earth melted. The LORD of hosts is with us; the God of Jacob is our refuge. Selah.

Chapter 9: How to maintain you

It starts with you, but it's never about you.

Every day is an opportunity given to you by God to live. It is very important to count it as blessing and never allow a day pass you by without discovering something new. How you carry yourself determines how far you will go.

Lamentations 3:22-23 - It is of the Lord's mercies that we are not consumed, because his compassions fail not. They are new every morning: great is thy faithfulness.

Matthew 5:16 - Let your light so shine before men, that they may see your good works, and glorify your Father which is in heaven.

Titus 2:7 - In all things shewing thyself a pattern of good works: in doctrine shewing uncorruptness, gravity, sincerity.

Colossians 3:23-24 - And whatsoever ye do, do it heartily, as to the Lord, and not unto men; Knowing that of the Lord ye shall receive the reward of the inheritance: for ye serve the Lord Christ.

Put you first in all

You can never give what you do not have. Always look at yourself beyond circumstances. Everything you go through is a lesson. Take some time and evaluate yourself. Look deeper than what pleases you. In most circumstances, people tend to do things that please others and they forget about themselves. In the end, they blame everyone for everything. But in reality, they had put themselves out of the equation. The best way to realize what needs to be changed in your life is to look up to people who have made it in life. Have a role model, and whoever you choose to look up to must challenge you, so that when you see them, you either want to be like them, more so, better than they are. It does not mean that you become a copycat of what they do. NO! You have to be inspired by them. Admire their courage, skill in doing things, and their attitude towards people who always want to pull them down.

You must never let anyone make you into what they want you to be in order to fit in their class. NO! You should be in position to identify who you are and start something new that will give you a unique identity.

Putting yourself first will cost you to an extent that you will need to cut off certain things that were not making *you* be, but instead, making you acceptable to others. Not that you should be selfish; be self-motivated. Go an extra mile and challenge yourself without anybody putting pressure on you.

Simple steps to put yourself first

Presentation (dressing): This gives you a personality before others, and a description. It's within human nature for people to judge others on first sight. As the saying goes, first impressions matter. Try as much as possible to know what looks good on you and is acceptable in society. Dress appropriately to glorify God so that when others see you, they respect you.

1 Corinthians 6:19 - What? know ye not that your body is the temple of the Holy Ghost [which is] in you, which ye have of God, and ye are not your own?

Romans 12:2 - And be not conformed to this world: but be ye transformed by the renewing of your mind, that ye may prove what is that good, and acceptable, and perfect, will of God.

The way you speak: A wise person does not talk all the time. You might end up saying things that are not meant for others to hear. People can easily tell your personality from the way you talk. It is not necessary for you to talk too much or dominate a conversation. Always try to be a listener; it's from the conversation of the other person that you can get a response. Give yourself a chance to internalize what is being said to you before you respond, and by the time you say anything, it comes out with wisdom.

James 1:19 - Wherefore, my beloved brethren, let every man be swift to hear, slow to speak, slow to wrath.

Mathew 12:37 - For by thy words thou shalt be justified, and by thy words thou shalt be condemned.

Self-control: This is a very important factor if you are to have healthy relationships. In most cases, what sparks off misunderstandings between people is when one does not know how to react to tight situations. If something unexpected happens to you, the best way to handle that situation is to take a few minutes and assess the whole situation. There are times when you do not need to react, depending on the situation, because if you are to do so, you will have yourself to blame, or others will even put the blame on you. So before reacting to anything, it is always wise and important to ask yourself questions like:

- How did this situation come about?
- What exactly sparked it to this level?

- Who is responsible for this situation?
- What were their intentions?
- How am I affected by this whole situation?
- How do I handle this, and where do I start?
- Who will understand me and stand with me?
- Am I meant to be part of what is going on?

Identify your strengths and weaknesses

In most cases, people tend to live in denial about who they are. If you explore the ins and outs of who you are, it puts you in a better situation to set goals, attain them, refrain yourself where you have to, and create boundaries where you need to.

Have you taken time to wholesomely look at yourself to find out what you are really good at? If not, take time and do so. You might be seated on a great potential which is meant to open so many good opportunities for you. It takes you to discover what you are good at. Discovering your strengths means working on them tirelessly to become an expert at them, which eventually makes you a pro.

Different people have different strengths in different fields. You might be doing something, and another person is doing the same thing, but there is always a time when you are preferred to the other person. That is why you should never allow fear get in your way, simply because you see other people doing the same thing you are doing. You need to have a unique brand that makes you preferred over others.

In the market place, different companies produce the same product, but brand it differently. Phones perform the same functions: calling and receiving calls, texting and taking pictures. But the manufacturers make them different in functionality by changing something slight like the camera, color, weight and buttons. All in all, they are all phones.

Invest more time in what you are doing, especially if it is for your good and the good of others. It should give you joy and peace. Be yourself, and be unique.

If you discover what you are not good at but you feel you can do it, do not fail to try. Practice makes perfect. Never be intimidated when you see others doing what you are interested in doing. Go for it, and be innovative.

Colossians 3:23 - And whatsoever ye do, do it heartily, as to the Lord, and not unto men; Knowing that of the Lord ye shall receive the reward of the inheritance: for ye serve the Lord Christ.

Proverbs 16:3 - Commit thy works unto the Lord, and thy thoughts shall be established.

Proverbs 12:24 - The hand of the diligent shall bear rule: but the slothful shall be under tribute.

Invest time in yourself

Take a good look at yourself; who do you see? Are you able to tell the difference between the you of today and the you of ten years back? The reason why I am posing these questions is to open your eyes to the fact that time matters. Every hour that passes by you is gone, but the way you chose to spend it determines how the next hour will be. It is easy to buy a new shirt and wear it for some time. All it takes is for you to wash it every time you take it off, so that it will be clean the next time you need it.

When it comes to time, it is not reversible. So, you need to use it wisely. Time moves with the day, a day moves with the week, a week moves with the month, and a month moves with the year. The experience of this week cannot determine your experience of next week, because you can never see through even the day you are in to the next day.

- It is very important to have a day's evaluation of self so that you are able to prepare for the next day accordingly. Of course, there will be unavoidable circumstances, some of which may not be pleasing to you, but the way you handle such situations can give you a pace of how to move on.

- If you are aware of something around you which does not benefit you, it is wise you let it go, because in the end you might blame the situation, yet you had the capacity to stay away. If it is hard for you to stay away, then seek help.

- The secret of your success is in looking further than the present and planning ahead. Although you may not know what will happen in the future, it's better to be prepared. Success meets preparation.

Ecclesiastes 3:1 - To everything there is a season, and a time to every purpose under the heaven.

Time does not lie, and time tells the story to others of who you are. People have a tendency of looking back in your life at things you achieved, and that is how man will always evaluate you. But glory be to God who qualifies you without consulting man or your past. You can make it; just be determined.

Chapter 10: Never give up

Everyone starts from somewhere: A place of uncertainty and doubt. No one wakes up and becomes successful all of a sudden. Working hard is the key, along with self-motivation and sacrifice. Just because someone close to you is doing better, it should not demoralize you from putting more effort in what you are doing.

It's very important to always look ahead to those who are successful and moving in a vision like the one you desire. The eye you use to look at them should have the perspective of learning and acquiring skill. Avoid the spirit of jealousy, because it will not allow you to improve; it only identifies the weaknesses that are in your role models.

Have a foundation

In most cases, a foundation is understood as the lowest load-bearing part of a building, typically below ground level. Also, a foundation can be understood as an idea, principles or base structure of an establishment like a business, organization or project which in the long run becomes big.

Every building has a foundation that determines the structure of that building. A thirty-story building cannot have a foundation of a five-story building, and a five-story building cannot have a foundation of a two-story building. This is the question I have for you. How big do you want your building to be? Have the foundation that will sustain it. And bear in mind as you start the foundation: keep the vision of the building so that you will use the right materials.

Luke 1:37 - For with God nothing shall be impossible.

2 Timothy 2:19 - Nevertheless the foundation of God standeth sure, having this seal, The Lord knoweth them that are his. And, let every one that nameth the name of Christ depart from iniquity.

As long as you put your trust in God and keep focused, that which you are dreaming of, will surely come to pass. When that time comes, others will ask this question: "How did you do it?"

Preparing a foundation

You need to see yourself way ahead of the foundation. Look at the finished product; it will give you a good layout of what kind of foundation you need to put down.

First things first

- Where do you see yourself years from now?

- Where do you see those you love and mean so much to you in the future?
- What kind of people do you want to take after you?
- What type of legacy do you want to leave behind you?

i.)   Prioritize your vision: you can never please everyone. So be prepared to be criticized by some people. It is one way you will actually be encouraged to work harder. When you become the head, definitely you become the headline. Therefore, choose to give your best to that vision you have and see to it that it will have an impact.

ii.)   Uniqueness gives identity. Do not do what others do, rather, do what others have not yet done, however much you got the idea from them. An idea can be gotten from someone else, but the implementation needs to be different - a mixture of different ideas. And the most important thing is to ask God for wisdom while you are laying down your foundation, based on your vision.

Proverbs 4:7 - Wisdom is the principal thing; therefore, get wisdom: and with all thy getting get understanding.

Basics of a foundation

Your success depends on these three things: People, Packaging, and Place (PPP). Having the right triple P's will take you to the top.

People

Like it or not, we all need people to stand with us in order to make that dream come true. However, there is a need to know what kind of people to keep around you, otherwise there are those who are with you, yet they are not for you. You need a discerning spirit to know people and understand their motives. Outside appearance is what people always use to determine who they keep around. Yet the inside of the person remains unknown, but can be discerned. As they say, don't judge a book by its cover, but remember to read the back cover.

What may seem undesirable is what sometimes can surprise you, and what may seem desirable can be a disappointment to you. So, as an entrepreneur and vision bearer, be extremely observant and prayerful. It is the only way you will be in position to keep the right people around you.

Keep in mind that people are like pages of a book. The book may be interesting, but you badly need to get to the conclusion, yet the story is still continuing. Every chapter comes with something new; it may not be what you expect, but that's what makes a book interesting, and keeps you reading.

Learn to live among and accommodate people, regardless of their status. You never know if the person you are despising may have that one thing you need to accomplish the foundation which will keep your vision alive.

Every individual carries a different attribute, and that's what makes the world interesting. Difference is like taste. Food tastes great when spiced well. Look at one's strengths, and at the same time their weaknesses, and use their strengths as long as they are for you to help build your foundation. Every stone is important; you just have to find where it fits best.

John 7:24 - Stop judging by mere appearances, but instead judge correctly (New International Version).

No man is an island. You cannot have everything you need by yourself satisfactorily. Man needs man in order to exist. We are created to complement each other, but not to compete. Okay, you are probably asking yourself, "How are we supposed to be better when we do not compete?" Competition is allowed, as long as the one you are competing with is not within your vision, but outside. When a person within your vision starts to compete with you, it's a big problem because they are going to cause your downfall. Know who to keep close and build that foundation with, in order to see your vision come to reality.

(Walk with those on the same mission with you.) An eagle cannot be in the company of chickens, simply because it soars high and has a clear vision from above. Yet a chicken keeps on the ground, and continually has to hide from the eagle to avoid being its prey.

So, the question I have for you is, "Who is that person close to you?" Are they helping you fly, or keeping you low, almost making you into prey (a failure)? Find the right company of people to support your vision, put the foundation together, and you will see the rise of that building.

Proverbs 13:20 - Walk with the wise and become wise, for a companion of fools suffers harm.

That person you constantly keep close to you will either build you or break you. You can identify yourself by looking closely at the company around you. Your growth is determined by the material imposed in you. It's high time you found yourself, because your identity is very important. No one can ever be you, though they can try to be like you.

Even if they do what you do, your unique touch makes all the difference. Strive to make people come after you, not you coming after people. Work to leave a footprint in life. Ancient buildings like Independence Hall in Philadelphia, PA, USA, the Texas State Capitol building in Austin, TX, USA, and the **Taj Mahal in India, are** landmarks.

You can make it and you will make it. It's high time you identified the right people to help you put up the right foundation in your life in order to live a legacy. It's never too late.

Packaging

For every piece of mail to be delivered well without any damage, it needs the right packaging. The way you present yourself before others will either usher you into the presence of great men, or keep you out.

It's very important to have the right people by you - people who can advise you accordingly and help you present yourself in an appropriate manner. Where there's a need to adjust and make things look better, you can, especially when you have a trustee that brings the right ideas to the table.

Remember, you are you, and you have no carbon copy. So, your dressing, eating, talking and listening skills are very important, because those are the attributes that make you.

Just like the foundation of a building, the measurements, quantity and quality of materials used is very important and should be taken seriously. Otherwise, if something goes wrong during the laying of a foundation, the building's longevity is compromised. After a certain period of time, it may collapse.

So, be yourself in all aspects and maintain you without allowing another person to impose their character onto you. Have principles of self and personal values.

Place

This is a very important aspect in life. Place can be understood in two ways. It can mean a position where you find yourself in life, or a practical place, location, or site you establish yourself in. There's a statement people usually use: "How did I get myself in this place?" In most cases, what someone is trying to express is, how did she or he make decisions up to this point where they have gotten into the situation they find themselves in? So, the statement comes out as a regret. However, it comes as a wake-up call for that particular person who suddenly makes it.

In life, people always work so hard to get to a place or a position. And for someone to attain that, there is a need to examine the people you surround yourself with. Like it or not, there are times when our decisions are based on the people we have close to us.

Your place in society can be determined by you. You need to get to a point of 'enough is enough' of where you are, and start attaining a higher position. As I wrote previously, it's important to know, love, accept and identify exactly who you are, without peer pressure. Being focused and determined can make you attain that place you desire and have always dreamed of.

The most important thing as you establish yourself is to identify a place which will accommodate what you are carrying inside of you, and ready to make it into manifestation. That place should be conducive and reciprocal. The structure you are looking forward to establishing, or method of implementation, should be easily adoptable by the natives of that place you are in. People are always attracted to something almost similar to what they are used to, though looking for uniqueness in it. Therefore, the best way to go about it is to learn the culture, values and norms of the people in a place you will be settling in to establish yourself.

You should be in a position to incorporate your skills within that place, without losing credibility and the originality of what you are bringing forth. A place greatly determines your growth or deterioration. Study the atmosphere before you establish yourself.

The greatest place to dwell in is the presence of God. There you will be able to get spiritual insight and direction on decision making. And when it comes to implementation, it will not be hard.

Psalm 91:1 - He that dwelleth in the secret place of the most High shall abide under the shadow of the Almighty.

Components of the foundation

- People do not need to see the foundation but one thing I am sure of, they will see the finished building.
- People will pass by the foundation, not having an idea of what the building will look like.
- Less or no attention is given to the foundation, yet a finished building draws attention.
- Your attitude during the foundation stages will determine the speed and rise of that project.

Keep on keeping on. Do not give up simply because some people do not understand you or do not support you. It's just a matter of time, and God will uplift you, and it only happens when you are diligent.

Psalm 118:22 - The stone which the builders rejected has become the chief cornerstone.

You may feel inferior if you pay attention to what others think and say about you. But as long as you block all the negative things said or spoken about you, your foundation is unstoppable. Have the 'I can do it' attitude; it will give you a push. People can have such a great influence on you, knowingly or unknowingly; they can make you, and at the same time, break you. The people who promise to always be by your side can easily walk away from you when you need them most. So put your trust in God.

Psalm 20:7 - Some trust in chariots, and some in horses: but we will remember the name of the Lord our God.

Deuteronomy 31:8 - And the LORD, he [it is] that doth go before thee; he will be with thee, he will not fail thee, neither forsake thee: fear not, neither be dismayed.

Start seeing value in yourself, and don't think about giving up on pursuing that which you keep envisioning as being yours. You have what it takes to cause a huge difference in so many other people's lives. Before you give up on yourself, remember: there are thousands that are meant to see you as their role models.

Philippians 4:13 - I can do all things through Christ which strengtheneth me.

Galatians 6:9 - And let us not be weary in well doing: for in due season we shall reap, if we faint not.

Chapter 11: Triple A

What you are about to read as I break down the triple A will open your eyes to the extent of making this scripture become alive in you.

Philippians 1:21 - For to me to live is Christ, and to die is gain.

The people you surround yourself with either pour into you or deduct from you. It is very important to die to self because it will resurrect the inner man who portrays the Christ in you. When you die to self, it is very easy to heal from the pain people cause you. In most cases, those you bring close to you are always the ones that cause you the inside wounds which man can never heal, but God can.

We need people and always will, but the question is, which kind of people can we bring close?

There are those who are near you but not close to you. Being near is knowing a bit about someone, like the car they drive, their place of residence, the church they attend and probably the kind of job they are doing. Yet being close is knowing so much about someone, to a point that you can even tell when they are not feeling well. Your close friend will know your secrets, the kind of perfume you wear, the places you go to, your favorite dish, the kind of music you love, the things you hate and those you love, your family members and part of your past, since you end up opening up to such a person. However, the more you open up, the more vulnerable you become to them.

That brings me to breaking down for you the triple A: Assistant, Assessor, and Assassin (AAA).

Assistant

This is a person who helps in a particular work, or ranks below a more senior individual. An assistant can also come in two other ways - a best friend or a company managing director who, in most cases, reports to the CEO. Looking at both of these parties, they tend to know so much about those they are close to or report to.

There's this other kind of assistant - a person who you come across and is meant to help you cross to the other side or connect you to other people who are to elevate you to another level. It becomes dangerous when you receive them as close friends meant to stay.

In my book *You Need a Jonathan*, I break down the different kinds of friends that cross our paths. There are four kinds. Winter friends, summer friends, spring friends and fall friends. All those friends come in different ways and for different purposes. That is why you need a spirit of discernment to differentiate an assistant from an assessor and assassin.

A true example of an assistant is found in the book of 1 Samuel 18. When Jonathan first met David, he saw beyond a man who had killed Goliath, to a point that Jonathan stripped himself of the robe that was upon him and gave it to David, along with his garments, sword, bow, and his girdle.

1 Samuel 18:1-4 - And it came to pass, when he had made an end of speaking unto Saul, that the soul of Jonathan was knit with the soul of David, and Jonathan loved him as his own soul. And Saul took him that day, and would let him go no more home to his father's house. Then Jonathan and David made a covenant, because he loved him as his own soul. And Jonathan stripped himself of the robe that was upon him, and gave it to David, and his garments, even to his sword, and to his bow, and to his girdle.

As long as Jonathan was alive, he stayed committed to David and defended him all the way so that his father Saul could not kill him. Jonathan saw the anointing on David, yet his father Saul saw him as a threat.

I have witnessed this being very common among friends, where one person sees the favor upon the other, and instead of riding on the same favor, they become jealous and start looking for ways of destroying them.

Therefore, it is very important to know that person close to you. Sometimes they keep around to take what belongs to you or destroy you.

Truthful assistants will always stand with you in the good, bad and ugly. The fact that they are always close to you means your interests should be their interests. If they are competitive, wanting to be better than you, then it's high time you got them out of your life before it's too late.

Assessor

This is a person who is knowledgeable, calculates, estimates or evaluates the quality of a person or thing. They usually take time assessing before taking action since they go into the nitty-gritty or details of things.

Some people close to you are assessors, not assistants. It is very important to train yourself on going slow with people, and when you start opening up, some personal details should be reserved. This will save you from future heartbreak and regret. So many times, we bring people close to us and get to trust them, not knowing their motives or hidden agenda.

Some assistants become assessors who eventually turn against you. They get to know so much about you, making it very easy for them to accomplish any of their plans, without putting you into consideration.

In any relationship, an assessor is empowered by the knowledge he/she has on the other person. That is to say, they look at your strengths and weaknesses, which makes it easier for them to get whatever they want, regardless of the situation the other person is in. Assessors' interests come first, and in most cases, they aim at getting you out of their way.

Assessors are usually insiders, the people you trust, believe in, open up to, and depend on. If your eyes do not open up to the real motives of the assessor, he/she can be your assassin.

Mathew 10:36 - And a man's foes shall be they of his own household.

Assassin

This is a murderer or killer of an important person in a surprise attack for either political, religious, business, or personal reasons.

Every person is important; it doesn't matter how others look at him or her. We are all created in

God's image and likeness, which gives all human beings a reason to live. So, no one has authority to take another person's life, no matter the circumstances.

The word assassin is used so much when the assassinated person is dead and no longer lives. But there are present assassins who can live with you, and you are as the walking dead. Whereby, you are still alive, yet the will to live is no longer present in you, because of the unseen septic wounds that you carry with you everywhere, and no human being is able to heal them.

It is easier to heal from a visible wound gotten from a car accident, than an invisible wound that you get when you are betrayed by a person you trusted most. Your flesh can heal and a scar is left, but your soul cannot easily heal when hurt unless touched by the Holy Spirit. Headache can be treated by pain killers, but heartache does not have pain killers. So many people walk with the unseen painful wounds caused by their assistants who assessed them, and later assassinated them.

You come across people making statements like:

- I can never trust anyone again.
- I will never fall in love again.
- I hate marriage.
- I hate men, or, I hate women.

- I will never help a stranger.
- I will never have a best friend.

All these statements are as a result of carrying unseen pain inside, to the point that it dictates the choices someone makes. There's a saying that experience is the best teacher. This applies both in positive and negative situations. If you've been bitten by a snake, the chances of you having one as a pet are next to impossible. You find that it is easy for people to forget the good times, but keep a good record of the bad.

This is a true story. I have a friend whose name I will conceal for reasons you will understand after reading this story. She hated men so much, to the point that it started bothering me. I kept asking her why, after noticing that she was getting worse, and hate was destroying her, too. And when she finally opened up to me, I couldn't resist the tears that were coming from my eyes. When she was eight years old, her mother invited a friend's son to stay with them as he was attending college, since they stayed close by. And almost every night he kept on going to her bed, and touched her private parts, while forcing her to touch his. She hated herself, and never ever wanted to even sit next to a boy in school. She told me that anytime a boy would come next to her, she would beat him up, and it's because she thought they were all the same. Unfortunately, she grew up with that hatred inside of her, and consistently condemned herself because she never told her mother about it. She was a born-again Christian and believed that was the best place to hide and stay away from men. After sharing with me, I asked her to allow me to pray for her. And once a week, we met to pray about it. For almost a year, it seemed so fresh that she hardly prayed, and only sobbed during prayer, because she had been carrying this pain with her for years. At the time I got to be friends with her, she was sixteen years old, and we started dealing with this when she was twenty-two years old. I thank God that I never gave up on her, but continually prayed for her, even in times she would not show up for prayers. After fourteen months she stopped coming over to my house or even speaking to me, which bothered me. But I kept her secret as she had asked me to. I started making her a priority every time I would go in prayer, because I didn't want to lose my friend, especially now when she was going through a tough time. The pain she had covered for years was now out, and she didn't know how to deal with it. I stood in the gap and knew prayer was the only answer.

I didn't hear from her or see her again, until four years later when we met at a wedding. (And) lo and behold, she did not come alone, but came with her husband and a baby boy. You can imagine my reaction. I shouted and hugged her about ten times, because I could not believe that she was married and had a child - a person who hated men! Her first words were, "Thank you for not giving up on me. I am free and not locked up in that cage you found me in."

That was a very big lesson for me not to judge people for their reactions, because you never know what someone is going through or went through that ended up giving them this personality, which is not the real them, but a cover up.

In this scenario my friend's trust of any man had been broken by a person whom she knew was meant to protect her, but instead abused her. So, he assassinated her trust and love, but glory be to God the restorer, she was able to love and trust again when she opened up and we prayed about the situation.

Never keep things to yourself that cause death to your inner man. Find that one person you look up to or trust and share, so that they can help you heal. It can be your father, mother, sister, brother, friend, or your pastor. Reach out for help before it's too late.

The situation may seem to be passive, but in the long run it can affect your behavioral pattern, or relationship with those that matter to you.

Even in the business sector, just because you had one business partner who betrayed you, doesn't mean that you should give up on starting another business. Not all people are evil; there's that one person God will connect you with to be your good Samaritan.

Luke 10:30-35 - And Jesus answering said, A certain man went down from Jerusalem to Jericho, and fell among thieves, which stripped him of his raiment, and wounded him, and departed, leaving him half dead. And by chance there came down a certain priest that way: and when he saw him, he passed by on the other side. And likewise a Levite, when he was at the place, came and looked on him, and passed by on the other side. But a certain Samaritan, as he journeyed, came where he was: and when he saw him, he had compassion on him, and went to him, and bound up his wounds, pouring in oil and wine, and set him on his own beast, and brought him to an inn, and took care of him. And on the morrow when he departed, he took out two pence, and gave them to the host, and said unto him, take care of him; and whatsoever thou spendest more, when I come again, I will repay thee.

Not everybody will notice what you are going through, and some who notice may even ignore you. One thing I want to assure you is, God has that one person he destined to help you. Put your trust in God and not in men. Men will walk away from you, but God will always be there to watch over you in the good and bad times.

Deuteronomy 31:6 - Be strong and of a good courage, fear not, nor be afraid of them: for the Lord thy God, he it is that doth go with thee; he will not fail thee, nor forsake thee.

Put this in mind: what some people meant for bad to destroy you, God will always turn it into good.

Romans 8:28 - And we know that all things work together for good to them that love God, to them who are the called according to his purpose.

It's high time you evaluated the people you surround yourself with. Some come for good and others for bad. So, ask God for a spirit of discernment to see people through spiritual eyes, rather than physical. The outside appearance in most cases is not the inside motive.

Never judge a book by its cover. Just as you may be walking with that unseen pain, so does someone else with hidden evil motives.

Watch your assistants. Some may be assessing you and will soon turn into assassins. You are different from everybody else, and so is everybody different from you. Therefore, learn to see people in different perspectives, giving yourself time to know them better before you fully open up to them.

Be yourself, not a carbon copy of someone else by taking up their character. Originals last, yet carbon copies fade.

Chapter 12: Stay original

Take a good look at yourself; there is nobody like you. And, the only way for you to understand that is when you appreciate everything about you. Nobody looks like you. If you come across someone with the same features as yours, it still does not make them you. Identical twins may look alike, but in most cases, they have different personalities, which makes them different.

Staying original means that you do not try to take up someone else's character in order to be like them. That gives you a challenge to discover who you are and develop that which you have discovered about yourself, and then start applying it in your life.

How to stay original

Never compromise

Compromise is to accept standards that are lower than what is desirable. As an individual, you need to have principles in life that you go by which help you in forming a unique identity that people describe you with. Your values and beliefs should mean so much to you that no matter what you do or where you go, you stand by them. You need to develop an attribute of standing on the truth. No matter what happens, never lower your standards to fit in with the crowd. It doesn't matter how long someone tries to compromise to have a sense of belonging; there will always be a feeling of low self-esteem, because reality will constantly hit them.

I have done a lot of counseling, especially with the youth, and the common thing among them all is looking for belonging, to the point that it makes them make bad choices, some of which they regret. The tendency of looking for acceptance usually causes people to compromise with their values and beliefs, and in the long run, they start condemning themselves for what they did.

Keep your standard and have self-discipline; that's the only way you will stay focused and see all your dreams come true.

Avoid being a people-pleaser

If you have a tendency of wanting everybody to be happy with you, then you need to stop. You can never please all. People are different; that is why you have probably been betrayed a number of times trying to make it up to everyone and forgetting about yourself.

Look at the life of Jesus Christ here on earth. He was there for people, as you read in the New

Testament. He performed miracles by healing the sick, raising the dead and feeding the hungry.

Matthew 14:13 - When Jesus heard of it, he departed thence by ship into a desert place apart: and when the people had heard thereof, they followed him on foot out of the cities. And Jesus went forth, and saw a great multitude, and was moved with compassion toward them, and he healed their sick. And when it was evening, his disciples came to him, saying, This is a desert place, and the time is now past; send the multitude away, that they may go into the villages, and buy themselves victuals. But Jesus said unto them, They need not depart; give ye them to eat. And they say unto him, We have here but five loaves, and two fishes. He said, Bring them hither to me. And he commanded the multitude to sit down on the grass, and took the five loaves, and the two fishes, and looking up to heaven, he blessed, and brake, and gave the loaves to his disciples, and the disciples to the multitude. And they did all eat, and were filled: and they took up of the fragments that remained twelve baskets full. And they that had eaten were about five thousand men, beside women and children.

Even after such a great miracle, when it came to the time of choice between him and a thief, these very people were asking for Barabbas the thief to be spared, in exchange for Jesus to be crucified.

So, you see, it's not about what you do for people. It's just a matter of time and they walk away from you, without caring how you feel or looking at the good things you did for them.

You can never know what is in the heart of man; that is why you need to be extremely careful when you go miles for people. But the most important thing is to always pray for those you love and cover them in the blood of Jesus so that they can stand strong in the times of trial, and pray against the spirit of betrayal.

Jeremiah 17:7 - The heart is deceitful above all things, and desperately wicked: who can know it?

Always do what is in your means and avoid trying to make everyone love you. The very people you sacrifice for to be happy can easily turn their backs on you, and you will see them no more. But there is one person I know who will never depart from you at all times, and that is Jesus Christ, the son of the living God. So, in all you do, please him, and you will never be disappointed.

Hebrews 13:5 - Let your conversation be without covetousness; and be content with such things as ye have: for he hath said, I will never leave thee, nor forsake thee.

Here is a secret. When you do something good for someone, don't sit there expecting a 'thank you,' because some people take love and kindness for granted. The more you eagerly wait for people to applaud you for the good you have done, the more you will hurt. Some people do not know how to love or receive love, and it's usually because of the circumstances they've gone through. Love has no meaning to them anymore. Character and reactions are greatly influenced by people's experiences, so when you help, give, or stand in the gap for someone, have a free spirit and don't attach yourself to what you have done. Move on, and God who sees in secret will surely reward you.

The more you please God, the more he will give you joy, and you will never be disappointed.

Don't talk unnecessarily

Words can build you or break you. Always watch what you speak, why you speak, to whom you are speaking, where you are speaking from, and the reason you are speaking. The words people hear have the power to impact them positively or negatively.

Therefore, you who is aiming at making a positive impact in the community and leaving a legacy for generations, you need to be extremely careful of the words that come out of your mouth. Ninety-five percent of the pain people carry around with them is caused by the words people have said to them.

People who talk a lot usually end up saying what they shouldn't have said. When talking, you need to listen to yourself, just like other people listening to you. The words you speak can be used against you if not properly and sensitively phrased. A person to whom something was said will always remember it, yet the one who said it can easily forget it. Relationships, businesses, marriages, families and churches are usually divided by the words people say.

This is a true story of a broken-hearted woman that I helped through counselling and prayers, to heal from pain that almost caused her to commit suicide. With her permission I am sharing this story, but concealing the name. I met her on one of the mission trips I do preaching the gospel. She came to me crying and full of hate for herself. It all started when her husband separated from her and left her with the children, who constantly asked her where their father was. Her husband found himself another young lady, whom he fell in love with and started telling lies about his wife, such as how she ignores him and spends most of her time in pursuing for further education, and working all the time. He kept telling people that she was wicked and evil and he couldn't stay with her any more. Her neighbors started avoiding her and whenever she went to church, people gave her a look of 'how dare you.' She couldn't understand why. Hate from people grew so much that no one wanted to talk to her, and she felt isolated and lonely. Even the people she thought were her friends stayed away from her. The situation made her get so confused that they even started calling her crazy, which made the situation worse for her. One day her pastor called her and began to ask her of all the wickedness he was told she does. The woman was in shock because she knew nothing of what the pastor was talking about. While narrating the story, she told me that she couldn't take in the questions from the pastor anymore, and that she just broke down before the pastor, crying, then walked out of his office without an explanation. Her husband had destroyed her so much with all the lies he spoke against her. She felt betrayed so much, yet she had sacrificed a lot for the family and her husband. Just because he fell in love with another young lady, he decided to destroy her by spreading lies about her. The pain she was going through was unbearable to watch as she cried uncontrollably. I prayed for her and the four days I had in their church ministering, I decided to have an hour with her every day. God, being faithful, slowly started healing her. I prayed for her to forgive her husband and release that pain in her inner man. It wasn't easy, but with the grace of God and the touch of the Holy Spirit she forgave him and was able to smile. A month later after I had left, she wrote to me and thanked me for creating time and speaking in her life. She told me that her husband had a big argument with the so-called girlfriend he had gone with, and they separated. He came back home and asked for her forgiveness. Thank God she had already released him from her spirit and forgiven him. And as I write this book, they are happily married, and the truth was finally known by the church community and their neighbors who had mistreated her.

It is never good running to conclusions because of the words you hear being said about someone. Sometimes people create lies and spread rumors about those they do not like. Words destroy families and cause community divisions. It calls for you who is reading this to be careful, starting from today, about what you say and hear.

Proverbs 10:19 - In the multitude of words there wanteth not sin: but he that refraineth his lips is wise.

Proverbs 18:21 - Death and life are in the power of the tongue: and they that love it shall eat the fruit thereof.

Proverbs 13:3 - He that keepeth his mouth keepeth his life: but he that openeth wide his lips shall have destruction.

Proverbs 21:23 - Whoso keepeth his mouth and his tongue keepeth his soul from troubles.

Before making a conclusion on someone they've told you about, do some investigation. Better still if you can, spend time with them if you are able to access them. From what they say, you will be able to know exactly who they are and assess whether what you were told is true or not.

When you avoid talking much, it protects you from being hurt. Sometimes people will take the very words they heard you speak, twist them around and use them against you. When you are quiet or say less, you will never empower others to destroy you. If you happen to have a friend that talks too much, be careful of what you tell them. The fact is that if they fail to keep their own secrets, how then will they keep your secrets? No matter the situation, try to speak with caution, because you never know how far what you have said will go.

Ephesians 4:29 - Let no corrupt communication proceed out of your mouth, but that which is good to the use of edifying, that it may minister grace unto the hearers.

Mathew 12:37 - For by thy words thou shalt be justified, and by thy words thou shalt be condemned.

Don't be a carbon copy

A carbon copy fades with time, however much it looks like the original. Do your best to stay in your lane to avoid collision. What I mean is, when you are yourself, you are able to set your own do's and don'ts, because you know the limits at which you can go. Every time you try to be someone else, you will wear out so fast, because you do not know what's behind the closets or what they do to appear the way they are. Seeing someone at face value is very different from knowing them. Your tastes and preferences are different from everyone else, so don't try to dress like somebody else, because your body structures are all different, especially with ladies. What looks good on the other person, may not look good on you. God created us unique from each other.

Never allow fear to stop you from being yourself. Every time you hold yourself back because you worry about what other people will say, you will definitely live as a coward and continue walking in other people's shadows.

When I was in high school, we had a book we were supposed to study in the history class, and unfortunately, I couldn't afford it at the time the teacher needed all of us to have it. So, I asked a friend to help me with hers, and every time we were starting a new chapter, I would go and make photocopies from her text book. What annoyed me was, at the end of the syllabus I had spent more than the actual book cost, and yet all my pages were scattered, simply because I had not put them in a binder. I regretted why I had not been patient enough to buy the book itself. So, what I did was to go buy the book in order to have it on me in preparation for my final exams.

Sometimes people waste so much time trying to duplicate what others have done, thinking they will be successful, yet it's time consuming. By the time they wake up, it's too late to catch up, and it's much more expensive. It's high time you started laying down a foundation according to your dreams and vision. Get out of the comfort zone and be creative. But most importantly, make sure you love, enjoy and stay focused; it's the only way you will build, protect, expand and have others admire your achievements.

If you have been struggling with identity, focus, and fear, go out there and start something of your own. It's time for your vision to come to life.

Joshua 1:9 - Have not I commanded thee? Be strong and of a good courage; be not afraid, neither be thou dismayed: for the LORD thy God is with thee whithersoever thou goest.

I know this book has not left you the same.

Read this prayer out loud.

Father, I come to you in the name of your son Jesus Christ. Forgive me of all my sins and iniquities. Thank you for loving me and giving me this opportunity to find myself and start living a life that will bring all the glory and honor to your name. From today, I refuse to be full of fear of the unknown and will never walk in the shadow of others. I ask you, Lord, to open my eyes, so that as I identify myself, I am able to love, embrace and accept that which is in and on me. Help me, Lord, adjust where I need to, and I receive a teachable spirit from those you are going to be directing to me as my destiny helpers.

Lord, I ask for wisdom and direction as I start my new beginning of living a life to its fullness, as I glorify your name. May you remove all those who have been a hindrance to my prosperity, and draining me instead of adding to me. Help me forgive all who hurt me in the time I was searching for my true identity.

I ask you, Lord, to bless the works of my hands, and help me be a blessing to those you will lead my way. From today, the old me is gone and the new me has come, in Jesus' mighty name. Amen.

2 Corinthians 5:17-18 - Therefore if any man be in Christ, he is a new creature: old things are passed away; behold, all things are become new. And all things are of God, who hath reconciled us to himself by Jesus Christ, and hath given to us the ministry of reconciliation.

As the author of this book, I thank you for purchasing and reading this life-transforming book, that I know has been an eye-opener. May the living God continue to bless you.